Tell Me A[ ]
Christmas

Christmas Coloring Book

Story based on Luke 1—2 and Matthew 1—2

Written by Robin Fogle

Illustrations by Mary Rojas

Warner
Press Kids™
educate • nurture • inspire
www.warnerpress.org

305800212096

Joseph and Mary loved God. They loved each other too.
Soon, they were going to get married.

Mary saw an angel. The angel said Mary was going to have a special baby. The baby was God's Son.

The king wanted to count his people.
Joseph and Mary had to take a long trip to Bethlehem.

The town was full of people. There was no room in the inn
for Mary and Joseph.

They had to sleep in the stable with the animals.

God's Son, Jesus, was born in the stable.

Mary wrapped Jesus in soft cloths to keep Him warm.

The animals ate their food from a manger.
Then Mary used it to make a little bed for Jesus.

Some shepherds were in the field near Bethlehem.

They were watching over their sheep at night.

Angels filled the sky. "Good news!
Today your Savior has been born!" they said.
The happy shepherds ran to see Him.

Joseph and Mary went to the temple.
They named Jesus and dedicated Him to God.

Later, wise men came from a land far away.

They followed a star to the house where Jesus was.

The wise men gave Jesus gifts. At Christmas
we give gifts to people we love too. We are happy
because Jesus is the best gift of all!